THE
CLASSIC BAR
& COCKTAIL BOOK

THE
CLASSIC BAR
& COCKTAIL BOOK

APPLE

JONATHAN GOODALL

A QUINTET BOOK

Published by The Apple Press
Sheridan House
112-116A Western Road
Hove
East Sussex BN3 1DD

ISBN 1-85076-861-7

Reprinted 1999, 2000, 2001

This book was designed and produced by
Quintet Publishing Limited
6 Blundell Street
London N7 9BH

Creative Director: Richard Dewing
Design: Deep Creative, London
Project Editor: Toria Leitch
Editor: Rosie Hankin
Photographer: Jeremy Thomas
Drinks Consultant: Phil Harradence

Typeset in Great Britain by Central Southern Typesetters, Eastbourne
Manufactured in Hong Kong by Regent Publishing Services Ltd
Printed in China by Leefung-Asco Printers Ltd

Please note a number of recipes in this book call for
uncooked eggs. Because of the slight risk of salmonella,
raw eggs should not be served to the very young, the ill
or elderly, or to pregnant women.

CONTENTS

INTRODUCTION

Shaken or stirred, straight up or on the rocks, with an olive or a twist? Cocktails are about choice. They're about choosing how to spend your precious time between winding down after work and the start of a seriously relaxing evening. They involve making a decision about hundreds of different spirits, liqueurs and mixers in thousands of colours and combinations. They are about choosing the company you wish to have to share intimate moments during the cocktail hour.

Cocktails are also about mixing. At a party, you might choose subconsciously who you wish to speak to, and who to avoid, on the basis of the cocktail they are clutching. Is it drop-dead cool and sophisticated, but perhaps a little too detached? Or is it frothy, gaudy, fizzy and vulgar, and just what you need after a tough day?

Nobody can really remember where or how cocktails originated, but that's hardly surprising when you consider what's in them. And how did they end up with such a peculiar name? Does it really come from the potent mixed drinks that were guzzled at cock-fighting tournaments? Or does it derive from the name for horses with clipped tails and mixed blood? Does it stem from a wine cup called *coquetel*? Is it something to do with Xoc-tl, the beautiful daughter of a Mexican king who would serve his guests with fiendish concoctions? Maybe the word really was coined by Elizabethan pirates who, making their way around the Caribbean, were treated to fiery drinks mixed with the slender root of a plant called *cola de gallo* (cock's tail).

Does it really matter? You decide. You choose.

THE ESSENTIAL
COCKTAIL KIT

You will need various combinations of the following tools to whip up your cocktails.

1 BOTTLE OPENER AND CORKSCREW

2 WAITER'S FRIEND: This clever device incorporates a corkscrew, bottle opener and knife in one cunning piece of kit.

3 CHOPPING BOARD AND PARING KNIFE: To cut twists of lemon and lime.

4 COCKTAIL STICKS: For skewering maraschino cherries and other things.

5 COCKTAIL STIRRERS: Often decorative, and left in the glass for the drinker to stir when required.

6 JUICE EXTRACTOR: Always a useful gadget.

7 BLENDER: This is necessary for certain mixing operations. I strongly advise against putting ice cubes in a standard blender if you value your blades.

8 SPIRIT MEASURE: You can gauge your measures by eye but a spirit measure might not be a bad idea. Feel free to amend the recipes to suit your taste.

9 SHAKER: Shaken cocktails are generally frothier affairs than the stirred variety because air is added. This also increases their volume. Using a shaker with cracked or crushed ice will produce a colder drink more quickly but can produce a more diluted cocktail as the ice gets more of a bashing and melts a bit faster. Glass shakers can obviate this to an extent as glass is a poorer heat conductor than metal.

7

5

4

8

10

6

the essential cocktail kit

10 MIXING GLASS AND LONG-HANDLED BAR SPOON: To keep a cocktail clear, if you are making a Dry Martini for instance, stir the ingredients in a mixing glass. Make sure you stir briefly and gently to avoid dilution and to retain effervescence if, for example, there is soda in the mixture.

11 STAINLESS STEEL STRAINER: A strainer is essential for keeping pieces of fruit and ice out of the glass when your cocktail is poured.

12 LARGE JUG: An alternative to a strainer could be a jug with a capacity of about 850 ml (1¹/₂ pints), with an involuted pourer to hold back the unwanted elements.

13 SODA BOTTLE: A bottle used for making soda water, which is forced out by pressure of gas.

14 ICE BUCKET: You will need plenty of ice, so keep an ice bucket to hand.

15 ICE CRUSHERS: Adjustable crushers will make cracked, crushed and shaved ice. Alternatively wrap the ice in a clean dish towel and then bash it with a kitchen mallet.

16 SUGAR SYRUP: Place equal quantities of sugar and water in a saucepan and bring to the boil. Reduce heat and simmer gently until the mixture condenses into a clear, sweet syrup, approximately 5 minutes. Cool. Use immediately or store indefinitely in a sealed container in the refrigerator.

9

G L A S S E S

A selection will add the aesthetic icing to the metaphorical cake. Place your glasses in the fridge for an hour before using them to chill them thoroughly.

SHOT GLASS: (capacity 30 to 50 ml/1 to 2 fluid ounces) A small glass used for cocktails that are taken in one mouthful.

HIGHBALL GLASS: (capacity 225 to 300 ml/ 8 to 10 fluid ounces) A multipurpose glass that comes in several alternative shapes.

COCKTAIL (MARTINI) GLASS: (capacity 125 to 300 ml/4 to 10 fluid ounces) A classic, long-stemmed glass, and a must for serving certain cocktails. The long stem is designed to keep your warm hand away from the bowl of the glass so your cocktail remains chilled until the final drop.

COLLINS GLASS: (capacity 300 to 450 ml/ 10 to 16 fluid ounces) This was specifically designed to accommodate the longest and tallest of cocktails.

OLD-FASHIONED GLASS: (capacity 125 to 225 ml/4 to 8 fluid ounces) A glass named after a type of cocktail, which is appropriate for any cocktail served on the rocks.

CHAMPAGNE FLUTE: This retains the sparkle in Champagne-based cocktails.

WINE GLASS: This is, strangely enough, best for wine-based cocktails.

WATER: Always drink plenty of water, about 1.2 l (2 pints), before you go to bed!

A N O T E A B O U T M E A S U R E S

As I have said, amend the recipes in this book to suit your taste. If you buy a spirit measure, it might have some strange words on it which I explain below. You might also meet unfamiliar measures in other recipes.

1 dash = 6 drops
3 teaspoons = 15 ml (1/2 fluid ounce)
1 pony = 30 ml (1 fluid ounce)
1 jigger = 40 ml (1 1/2 fluid ounces)
1 large jigger = 50 ml (2 fluid ounces)

1 standard whisky glass = 50 ml (2 fluid ounces)
1 pint = 600 ml (20 fluid ounces)
1 fifth = 900 ml (32 fluid ounces)
1 quart = 1.2 litres (2 pints)

the essential cocktail kit

SHOT GLASS   SHOT GLASS   SHOT GLASS

HIGHBALL GLASS   OLD-FASHIONED GLASS   ROCKS GLASS

HIGHBALL GLASS   SLING GLASS   WINE GLASS

CHAMPAGNE FLUTE   COCKTAIL (MARTINI) GLASS   MARGARITA GLASS

BRANDY

BETWEEN THE SHEETS

- **50 ml (2 fl oz) brandy**
- **50 ml (2 fl oz) light rum**
- **40 ml (1¹/₂ fl oz) lemon juice**
- **30 ml (1 fl oz) Cointreau or Triple Sec**
- **Twist of lemon or lime peel**

Shake ingredients with ice then strain into a cocktail glass. Slide in.

brandy cocktails

BRANDY ALEXANDER

- 50 ml (2 fl oz) brandy
- 30 ml (1 fl oz) dark crème de cacao
- 30 ml (1 fl oz) double cream
- Pinch of grated nutmeg

Shake ingredients with ice, before straining into a cocktail or Champagne glass, and decorating with nutmeg.

BRANDY GUMP

- 50 ml (2 fl oz) brandy
- Juice of 1 lemon
- Dash of grenadine

As the name might suggest, simple but quite zippy. Shake with ice and strain into a frosted cocktail glass.

CLASSIC

- 50 ml (2 fl oz) brandy
- 30 ml (1 fl oz) curaçao
- 30 ml (1 fl oz) maraschino liqueur
- 30 ml (1 fl oz) lemon juice
- Maraschino cherry or twist of lemon

Shake ingredients with ice then strain into a frosted cocktail glass. Serve with a succulent maraschino cherry impaled on a cocktail stick, or a twist of lemon.

DEPTH CHARGE

- 50 ml (2 fl oz) brandy
- 30 ml (1 fl oz) calvados
- 50 ml (2 fl oz) lemon juice
- 30 ml (1 fl oz) grenadine
- Twist of lemon

Shake ingredients with ice. Strain into a cocktail glass and hang a twist of lemon on the rim. Delivers quite a revitalizing blast to the stomach.

DIZZY DAME

- 50 ml (2 fl oz) brandy
- 30 ml (1 fl oz) cherry brandy
- 30 ml (1 fl oz) Kahlúa
- 50 ml (2 fl oz) double cream
- Maraschino cherry

Shake ingredients with ice and pour into the anticipating tumbler. Serve up with a maraschino cherry. Dizzy by name...

FOXHOUND

- 50 ml (2 fl oz) brandy
- 1 measure cranberry juice
- 30 ml (1 fl oz) Kümmel (German caraway seed liqueur)
- Dash of lemon juice
- Slice of lemon

Shake ingredients with ice then serve in a tumbler. Decorate with a slice of lemon. Within the hunting fraternity, when the chase is over, this little snapper is traditionally served before game dishes.

MAE WEST

- 50 ml (2 fl oz) brandy
- ¹/₂ egg yolk
- 2.5 ml (¹/₂ tsp) sugar
- Pinch of cayenne pepper

Shake ingredients with ice then strain into a frosted cocktail glass. Break the ice with a sprinkling of cayenne. Hot with plenty of body.

METROPOLITAN

- 40 ml (1¹/₂ fl oz) brandy
- 50 ml (2 fl oz) vermouth
- Dash of Angostura bitters
- Dash of sugar syrup

Shake the little devil with ice. Strain into a frosted cocktail glass. As sophisticated as it sounds.

MOULIN ROUGE

- *50 ml (2 fl oz) brandy*
- *125 ml (4 fl oz) fresh pineapple juice*
- *Top up with chilled Champagne or sparkling white wine*

Pour the brandy and pineapple juice over a few blocks of ice in a Highball glass. Splash in the fizz.

NEVER ON SUNDAY

- *50 ml (2 fl oz) Greek brandy*
- *30 ml (1 fl oz) ouzo*
- *Dash of lemon juice*
- *Dash of Angostura bitters*
- *Top up with chilled Champagne and/or ginger beer*

Stir all ingredients, except the Champagne and ginger beer, in a mixing glass. Pour into a Highball glass then drench it with the Champagne/ginger beer combo. In retrospect, Sunday is probably the best day for this drink.

SIDECAR

- *50 ml (2 fl oz) brandy*
- *30 ml (1 fl oz) Cointreau or Triple Sec*
- *2 dashes of lemon juice*
- *Twist of lemon*

Shake ingredients well with a few blocks of ice and strain into a chilled cocktail glass. Decorate with lemon peel.
  According to cocktail folklore, this libation is named after the mode of transport by which the soldier, for whom it was first made, would arrive at his favourite Paris bar during the First World War. Careful how you take those corners.

YANKEE PRINCE

- *30 ml (1 fl oz) apricot brandy*
- *30 ml (1 fl oz) yellow Chartreuse*
- *30 ml (1 fl oz) Pernod*

Shake with ice and strain into a chilled cocktail glass. Yeeha!

CAMPARI

AMERICANO

- **50 ml (2 fl oz) Campari**
- **50 ml (2 fl oz) sweet vermouth**
- **Top up with chilled club soda**
- **Slice of orange**

Stir the Campari and vermouth in an ice-filled tumbler or Old-fashioned glass. Add soda to taste. Slide the orange slice over the lip of the glass. As thirst-quenching as a cocktail can get.

campari cocktails

NEGRONI

- **30 ml (1 fl oz) Campari**
- **30 ml (1 fl oz) gin**
- **30 ml (1 fl oz) sweet vermouth**
- **Twist of lemon**

Stir the Campari, gin and vermouth with some ice in a mixing glass. Serve in a cocktail glass, decorated with the lemon twist.

PINK PUSSY CAT

- **50 ml (2 fl oz) Campari**
- **30 ml (1 fl oz) peach brandy**
- **Dash of egg white**
- **Top up with chilled Collins mix (juice of 1 lemon, 5 ml (1 tsp) sugar, soda)**

Mix the Campari, peach brandy and egg white with ice in a shaker then strain into a Highball glass. Top up with Collins mixture. Depending on the amount of Collins mixture you use, this cocktail is as long, tall and refreshing as you wish it to be.

CHAMPAGNE
& SPARKLING WINE

BELLINI

- **3 or 4 peaches or peach juice**
- **1 bottle chilled Champagne**

If you are using fresh peaches these should be stoned and puréed in a blender with some ice cubes. Alternatively, follow the same procedure with peach juice/nectar. Transfer to a punch bowl and stir in the Champagne. Serve in Champagne flutes or large goblets.

Equally delicious is a mango Bellini where the peaches are substituted for mango. Make sure the fruit is ripe.

This cocktail originates from Harry's Bar in Venice, a popular watering-hole among film stars in the sixties.

BLACK VELVET

- *Half chilled Guinness (or any other stout)*
- *Half chilled Champagne*

Pour the chilled Guinness and Champagne into a large punch bowl. Do not stir. You might need a sympathetic friend to help you with this one as the two drinks should be poured simultaneously. Pour into very tall glasses and savour the silkiest, smoothest bubbles you will ever swallow.

CHAMPAGNE BUCK

- *50 ml (2 fl oz) Champagne*
- *30 ml (1 fl oz) gin*
- *2 dashes of cherry brandy*
- *5 ml (1 tsp) orange juice*

How to make a fast buck. Give ingredients a hefty shake with ice then strain the effervescent mixture into a cocktail glass. A quick buck with your partner can pep you up no end.

CHAMPAGNE CHARLIE

- *50 ml (2 fl oz) apricot brandy*
- *Top up with chilled Champagne*

How about pouring the apricot brandy into a Champagne flute and topping it up with chilled Champagne? Dead simple and taking its name from the legendary lush about town.

CHAMPAGNE COCKTAIL

- *1 sugar cube*
- *Approximately 3 drops Angostura bitters*
- *30 ml (1 fl oz) brandy (optional)*
- *Top up with chilled Champagne*
- *Slice of orange (optional)*

A classic classic. Place sugar cube in a Champagne flute and soak it in Angostura. If you need the reinforcement of brandy, pour this over the sugar cube before the Champagne topping-up operation. Add a bit of zest with an orange slice if you want to live dangerously.

DEATH IN THE AFTERNOON

- *30 ml (1 fl oz) pastis*
- *Top up with chilled Champagne*

Guess what. Pour the pastis into a Champagne flute before topping it up with Champagne. Contrary to popular opinion, this cocktail is no worse for you than any other if you face a hectic afternoon. Drinking any alcoholic cocktail at lunchtime will affect your P.M.P. (Post Meridian Performance).

INDEPENDENCE DAY PUNCH

- *Juice of 12 lemons*
- *900 g (2 lb) icing sugar*
- *600 ml (1 pt) strong tea*
- *3 bottles dry red wine*
- *1 bottle brandy*
- *1 bottle chilled Champagne*
- *Lemon slices*

Declare your independence on 4 July with this summertime punch. Pour the lemon juice and sugar into a punch bowl. Make sure the sugar is dissolved. Throw in some ice cubes and pour in the tea, red wine and brandy. Place in the fridge to chill. Add the Champagne just before serving to give it that extra fizz. Serve in goblets decorated with lemon slices.

KIR ROYALE

- *Maraschino cherry*
- *30 ml (1 fl oz) crème de cassis*
- *Top up with chilled Champagne*
- *Strawberry*

Drop the cherry into the bottom of a Champagne flute and pour the crème de cassis over. Top up with Champagne. Garnish your blackcurrant flavoured fizz with a sliced strawberry pushed over the rim of the glass. A delicious fruity concoction.

NEW ORLEANS DANDY

- *50 ml (2 fl oz) light rum*
- *30 ml (1 fl oz) peach brandy*
- *Dash of orange juice*
- *Dash of lime juice*
- *Slice of orange*
- *Maraschino cherry*

Pour the rum and peach brandy into a shaker. Politely introduce the dashing orange and lime juice and a few chunks of reserved, stand-offish ice. Set them all talking with a vigorous shake and decant to a Highball glass. Decorate with a flourish of orange and a maraschino cherry.

RITZ FIZZ

- *2 dashes of blue curaçao*
- *Dash of amaretto*
- *Dash of lemon juice*
- *Top up with chilled Champagne*
- *Rose petal (optional)*

If you pine for blue Champagne with a sweetish hint of almonds, then this one's for you. Stir the curaçao, amaretto and lemon juice in a goblet. Top up with Champagne. You can float an upturned rose petal on top if you're serving it to a loved one. You could always present what's left of the rose, providing of course the petal extraction has inflicted the minimum damage. Handy hint: If you're going to all this trouble it might be a good idea to strain the lemon juice so that unsightly floating bits don't spoil the special moment.

DUBONNET

DUBONNET FIZZ

- 50 ml (2 fl oz) Dubonnet
- 5 ml (1 tsp) cherry brandy
- Juice of ¹/₂ lemon
- Juice of ¹/₂ orange
- Top up with chilled soda

Shake all but the soda with plenty of ice and strain into a Highball glass for a sweet fruity cocktail.

dubonnet cocktails

LOUISIANA LULLABY

- *10 ml (2 tsp) Dubonnet*
- *50 ml (2 fl oz) dark rum*
- *Dash of Grand Marnier*
- *Lemon peel*

Stir the ingredients
with ice and strain into
a cocktail glass. Decorate
with lemon peel, cut into
the shape of a star. Take a
snooze on the porch.

MAYFLOWER

- *50 ml (2 fl oz) Dubonnet*
- *30 ml (1 fl oz) brandy*

Shake the Dubonnet and brandy with ice
and strain into a chilled cocktail glass.
The brandy gives quite a kick to the
quinine flavour of the Dubonnet and
would have warmed the barnacles of the
Pilgrim Fathers on their arduous ocean
crossing, though I doubt Dubonnet was
widely available in those days.

MERRY WIDOW

- *50 ml (2 fl oz) Dubonnet*
- *50 ml (2 fl oz) dry vermouth*
- *Dash of orange bitters*
- *Twist of lemon*

Stir the Dubonnet and dry vermouth with
ice and strain into a cocktail glass. Dash
in the orange bitters and add lemon peel.

There are various twists on the Merry
Widow theme. A quite different, though
equally merry, alternative is made with
30 ml (1 fluid ounce) of cherry brandy and
30 ml (1 fluid ounce) of maraschino liqueur
(*instead* of the Dubonnet and vermouth)
and the cocktail is then decorated with
cherries—use fresh or maraschino.

GIN

ALASKA

- **50 ml (2 fl oz) gin**
- **15 ml ('/₂ fl oz) green Chartreuse**
- **30 ml (1 fl oz) dry sherry (optional)**
- **Twist of lemon**

Stir the ingredients with ice cubes then strain into a cocktail glass. Decorate with the lemon twist. Chill out. If you decide to include the sherry the resulting cocktail is known as a Nome.

You could use yellow Chartreuse for this cocktail but the green version is much drier, more aromatic and less plain sickly.

gin cocktails

BROADWAY SPECIAL

- *50 ml (2 fl oz) gin*
- *30 ml (1 fl oz) sweet vermouth*
- *5 ml (1 tsp) pineapple juice*
- *2 dashes of grenadine*
- *¹/₂ egg white*
- *Pinch of grated nutmeg*

Shake ingredients with ice and strain into a chilled cocktail glass. Add some fresh pineapple for a big production number.

BRONX

- *50 ml (2 fl oz) gin*
- *15 ml (¹/₂ fl oz) dry vermouth*
- *15 ml (¹/₂ fl oz) sweet vermouth*
- *15 ml (¹/₂ fl oz) orange juice*
- *Slice of orange*

Shake the lot with ice cubes and strain into a wine glass. This could also be served on the rocks in an Old-fashioned

glass. Decorate with a slice of orange.

For a drier style, leave out the sweet vermouth and use 30 ml (1 fluid ounce) of dry. The addition of an egg yolk transforms this into a Golden Bronx; the addition of an egg white makes it a Silver Bronx; and an infusion of blood orange instead of orange orange renders a Bloody Bronx.

DRY MARTINI

- *1 cocktail glass of gin*
- *Dash of dry vermouth*
- *Dash of orange bitters (optional)*
- *Twist of lemon peel*

Arguably the most satisfying apéritif but strewn with social pitfalls. Stir the gin and vermouth (and orange bitters if desired) with ice in a mixing glass. Strain into a chilled cocktail glass. Twist the lemon peel, skin-side down, over the drink before dropping it in. This releases a fine spray of zest on to the surface which helps to produce the Martini's oily appearance. You could decorate this cocktail with an olive instead of lemon peel. Small cocktail onions may also be used in a Dry Martini, the number used varying from 1 to 3. The result of this particular decoration is called a Gibson.

There is another, equally socially acceptable way to make a Dry Martini which involves rinsing the inside of the cocktail glass with dry vermouth, pouring it back in the bottle and topping up the glass with iced gin.

So much has been written about the 'correct' gin/vermouth ratio that one is reminded of Jonathan Swift's Lilliputians going to war over the 'correct' end to open an egg. Brazen show-offs afflicted by cocktail machismo will tell you that as much as 15 parts gin to one part vermouth is the right proportion, but the original Martini was made with half and half, sometimes using sweet vermouth. Today, cocktail bars are likely to offer Dry Martinis ranging from three parts gin/one part vermouth to six parts gin/one part vermouth.

FLUFFY DUCK

- 50 ml (2 fl oz) gin
- 50 ml (2 fl oz) advocaat
- 30 ml (1 fl oz) Cointreau
- 30 ml (1 fl oz) orange juice
- Slice of orange
- Maraschino cherry
- Top up with chilled soda

Pour the ingredients into a glass filled with ice, stir and top up with soda. It's not fluffy and there's no duck in it.

ACM GELARDI MARTINI

- 50 ml (2 fl oz) gin
- 15 ml (¹/₂ fl oz) Cointreau
- Dash of lemon juice
- 5 or 10 ml (1 or 2 tsp) orange marmalade, according to taste
- Slices of orange

This strangely named Martini (sometimes called a Breakfast Martini) takes its name from the great grandfather of Geoffrey Gelardi who is the managing director of The Lanesborough in London. The slightly bitter flavour of the marmalade mixes extremely well with the juniper content of the gin.

Place all the ingredients in a shaker with some ice. You need to give this one a particularly sharp shake-up in order to combine the marmalade properly. Pour it through a strainer into a chilled cocktail glass. You might like to decorate it with a slice of orange but to be honest it doesn't really need it.

GIMLET

- 30 ml (1 fl oz) gin
- 15 ml (¹/₂ fl oz) lime cordial

Shake the gin and lime cordial with ice and strain into a cocktail glass.

For a longer, more refreshing version of this classic cocktail—sometimes referred to as either a Gimlet Highball or, less formally, as a Rickey—mix 50 ml (2 fluid ounces) of gin, 30 ml (1 fluid ounce) of fresh lemon or lime juice and a dash of grenadine with ice in a Highball or Old-fashioned glass. Top up the glass with soda and stir clockwise. If you find it a little bitter, add sugar to taste.

gin cocktails

GINGER ROGERS

- 30 ml (1 fl oz) gin
- 30 ml (1 fl oz) apricot brandy
- 30 ml (1 fl oz) dry vermouth
- Dash of lemon juice
- Maraschino cherry

Shake with ice. Strain into a chilled cocktail glass and serve up with a maraschino cherry. Step out.

GIN 'N' SIN

- 1 cocktail glass of gin
- 5 ml (1 tsp) lemon juice
- 5 ml (1 tsp) orange juice
- Dash of grenadine

Stir the gin, fruit juices and grenadine with ice in a mixing glass. Strain into a cocktail glass. Naughty but nice.

The notorious Gin 'n' It is made in the same way using roughly three parts gin to one part vermouth in place of the fruit juices and grenadine.

JET BLACK

- 50 ml (2 fl oz) gin
- 10 ml (2 tsp) black sambuca
- 5 ml (1 tsp) sweet vermouth
- Maraschino cherry
- Slice of lemon

Stir with ice in a mixing glass before straining into a cocktail glass.

A great cocktail for the poseur who wants everyone to be wondering what on earth they're drinking. Let's face it, you don't see many black drinks.

MAIDEN'S BLUSH

- 50 ml (2 fl oz) gin
- 4 dashes of orange curaçao
- 4 dashes of grenadine
- Dash of lemon juice
- 5 ml (1 tsp) sugar (optional)
- 5 ml (1 tsp) raspberry syrup (optional)
- Slice of lemon

Shake ingredients with ice and strain into a cocktail glass. The raspberry syrup will make your Maiden's Blush a little deeper.

ORANGE BLOSSOM

- 50 ml (2 fl oz) gin
- Juice of ½ orange
- 5 ml (1 tsp) sugar
- Slice of orange

Shake ingredients with ice and serve in a chilled cocktail glass. Decorate with an orange slice.

SINGAPORE SLING

- 20 ml (²/₃ fl oz) gin
- 20 ml (²/₃ fl oz) cherry brandy
- 10 ml (¹/₃ fl oz) Cointreau
- 10 ml (¹/₃ fl oz) Benedictine
- 10 ml (¹/₃ fl oz) lime juice
- 75 ml (2¹/₂ fl oz) orange juice
- 75 ml (2¹/₂ fl oz) pineapple juice
- Slice of pineapple

Shake all ingredients with ice. Strain into a Highball or Collins glass over ice and decorate with a slice of pineapple.

A simpler version uses 40 ml (1¹/₂ fluid ounces) of gin, 20 ml (²/₃ fluid ounce) of cherry brandy, and 20 ml (²/₃ fluid ounce) of lemon juice, mixed together and topped up with soda.

SLOE GIN

- **30 ml (1 fl oz) sloe gin**
- **15 ml (¹/₂ fl oz) dry vermouth**
- **Dash of Angostura bitters**

Stir ingredients in a mixing glass with some ice then strain into a cocktail glass. A dry version of this drink can be made by doubling the dry vermouth content, while a sweet version can be made by using sweet vermouth at the expense of the dry.

Sloe gin is flavoured with the small, sour, blue-black fruit of the blackthorn (called the sloe berry).

THANKSGIVING COCKTAIL

- 30 ml (1 fl oz) gin
- 30 ml (1 fl oz) dry vermouth
- 30 ml (1 fl oz) apricot brandy
- Dash of lemon juice
- Maraschino cherry

Shake with ice cubes and strain into a cocktail glass. Decorate with a cherry. It might be appropriate to try one of these after trying a Mayflower (see page 25).

TOM COLLINS

- 85 ml (3 fl oz) gin
- Juice of 1 lemon
- 5–10 ml (1–2 tsp) sugar, to taste
- Top up with chilled soda
- Slice of orange or lemon

Stir ingredients with ice cubes in a large Highball or Collins glass. Top up with soda. Stir again and decorate with orange or lemon slice. Hell, you could use both and even throw in a cherry.

Collinses are the longest and tallest of long tall drinks. They are so long and tall in fact that the Collins glass, which holds anything between 300 and 450 ml (10 and 16 fluid ounces), was invented for them. Collinses could be described as spiked lemonade. They are scintillatingly refreshing in hot weather. While the gin-based Tom Collins is the most common incarnation, there are as many types of Collinses as there are types of spirit. A Pedro Collins uses rum, a Pierre Collins uses brandy and a John Collins uses bourbon. Get the picture?

ZA ZA

- Dash of Angostura bitters
- 50 ml (2 fl oz) gin
- 50 ml (2 fl oz) Dubonnet
- Twist of lemon peel

Splash the Angostura into a mixing glass then pour in the gin and Dubonnet. Stir and strain into a cocktail glass. Decorate with lemon peel.

LIQUEURS

B - 5 2

- *30 ml (1 fl oz) Kahlúa*
- *30 ml (1 fl oz) Bailey's Irish Cream*
- *30 ml (1 fl oz) Grand Marnier*

Carefully layer each liqueur in a small shot glass, to make three distinctive layers. For added effect, turn out the lights and ignite the Grand Marnier. (Caution: extinguish before you drink it!)

CREOLE COCKTAIL

- 30 ml (1 fl oz) Malibu
- 30 ml (1 fl oz) orange juice
- 30 ml (1 fl oz) vodka
- Dash of grenadine
- Slice of orange
- 2 slices of coconut

Give the ingredients a good shake, pour into a large ice-filled goblet and decorate with the orange and coconut slices.

SAINT CHRISTOPHER

- 30 ml (1 fl oz) chocolate liqueur
- 30 ml (1 fl oz) Bacardi
- 1/8 of fresh melon
- 5 ml (1 tsp) chocolate powder
- 5 ml (1 tsp) sugar syrup (to taste)
- 50 ml (2 fl oz) milk
- Chocolate flake and 2 fresh mint leaves

This one's ridiculously easy to make, providing you own a blender which is robust enough to deal with ice cubes. Peel and seed the melon then put all the ingredients with six ice cubes into a blender. Flick the switch. Pour the frothy mixture into a tall glass and decorate with a chocolate flake and a couple of fresh mint leaves.

In case you're wondering, the barman who created this chocolate extravaganza is called Christopher. The 'Saint' was added ironically because you can barely taste any alcohol, making Saint Christopher a bit of a time-bomb. Sip with caution and dream chocolate dreams.

KAHLÚA CAFÉ DON JUAN

- **Brown sugar**
- **Wedge of lemon**
- **15 ml (¹/₂ fl oz) dark rum**
- **30 ml (1 fl oz) Kahlúa**
- **Hot coffee**
- **Double cream**
- **Grated chocolate**

End the evening with this hot flush of a cocktail, but make sure your household

contents insurance is fully paid up before you start. We begin by frosting the rim. Pour the brown sugar into a dish which is wide enough to accommodate an upturned large goblet. Squeeze then wipe the lemon wedge around the rim of the goblet. Gravity dictates that if the goblet is held upside-down the lemon juice won't trickle into it. Dip upturned goblet into the dish of sugar. This could take several attempts. A similar effect can be achieved by using caster sugar affixed with egg white, though brown sugar is preferable for this recipe. Some cocktail recipes advocate colouring caster sugar with various cordials and fruit-based liqueurs and dyes before frosting the glass and then drinking the concoction through a straw so as not to mess up your artistic endeavours, but this is entering into the realms of the truly precious.

Right, you've frosted the goblet. Pour in the rum and set fire to it before swirling it around (I warned you to check up on your insurance). Extinguish any fires that might have started, then pour in the Kahlúa. Top up with hot coffee. If you have any enthusiasm or energy left, carefully pour the cream over the back of a teaspoon onto the molten surface of your 'drink'. Sprinkle grated chocolate over the top.

MELON SOUR

- **30 ml (1 fl oz) melon liqueur**
- **50 ml (2 fl oz) lemon juice**
- **1 egg white**
- **2 melon balls**
- **Maraschino cherry**

Here's a good way to use up that melon liqueur your aunt bought you. Shake said liqueur with the lemon juice, egg white and cracked ice until frothy. Strain into a small goblet. Give full vent to your creative side by skewering the two melon balls, with the cherry in between, with a cocktail stick. Balance across the rim of the glass.

POUSSE-CAFÉ

- *Grenadine (red)*
- *Crème de cacao (brown)*
- *Crème de menthe (green)*
- *Parfait Amour (violet)*
- *Maraschino liqueur (white)*
- *Orange curaçao (self-explanatory)*
- *Brandy (you know its colour)*

The ultimate cocktail balancing act, this one's for congenital (or congenial) show-offs. It is made more to be admired than consumed. There are countless variations on the Pousse-Café theme, but they all produce a traffic-light effect of layered liqueurs, on top of one another.

For fairly obvious reasons, you will need a tallish straight-sided glass for this one. I have listed the recommended ingredients in the order in which they are to be poured carefully over the back of a teaspoon into the glass. Those with the heaviest density (generally those with the most sugar content and lowest or no alcohol content) are poured first to allow them to settle in the bottom of the glass. The obverse applies.

This is more of a party game than a drink, so you can experiment with different densities to your heart's content (or until you get bored). Remember, any sudden movements could spoil the overall effect, so treat each ingredient as if it were nitroglycerin and you should be okay.

SEX ON THE BEACH

- *30 ml (1 fl oz) peach schnapps*
- *30 ml (1 fl oz) vodka*
- *50 ml (2 fl oz) orange juice*
- *50 ml (2 fl oz) cranberry juice*
- *Maraschino cherry*
- *Slice of orange*

In contrast to most of these liqueur-based cocktails, you might like to try drinking this one. Pour all the ingredients into a Highball glass containing ice. Stir well and decorate with the cherry and orange slice. Omitting the cranberry juice renders a Fuzzy Navel.

PERNOD

I'm prepared to venture that any of these Pernod-based cocktails could use anisette (a clear liqueur made from the anise seed and flavoured with bitter almonds and coriander) instead of Pernod. But I'm not prepared to suggest that you try substituting Pernod for Greek ouzo for fear of waking up to find a frog's head on my pillow.

Historical footnote: Absinthe, which is now illegal in most countries, is an anise-flavoured drink which originated in Switzerland and was popular among the more bohemian of European artists up until the end of the nineteenth century. Its manufacture was banned after it was suspected of leading to dependency, madness and infertility—a pretty bad press, even by today's standards. Little is known of any other side-effects, though the paintings of Edvard Munch could provide a few clues.

MORNING CALL

- *30 ml (1 fl oz) Pernod*
- *15 ml (¹/₂ fl oz) maraschino liqueur*
- *15 ml (¹/₂ fl oz) lemon juice*

Start the day as you mean to go on.
Shake ingredients with ice and strain into a chilled cocktail glass.

YANKEE PRINCE

- *30 ml (1 fl oz) Pernod*
- *30 ml (1 fl oz) apricot liqueur*
- *30 ml (1 fl oz) yellow Chartreuse*

Shake ingredients with ice and strain into a chilled cocktail glass.

ZERO COCKTAIL

- *30 ml (1 fl oz) Pernod*
- *5 ml (1 tsp) grenadine*
- *10 ml (2 tsp) orange juice*

Shake ingredients with ice and strain into a chilled cocktail glass.

RUM

ACAPULCO

- 40 ml (1¹/₂ fl oz) light rum
- 30 ml (1 fl oz) Cointreau
- 85 ml (3 fl oz) pineapple juice
- 30 ml (1 fl oz) lime juice
- Cubed pineapple (optional)

Shake the ingredients with ice and serve in a Collins glass, decorated with pineapple cubes.

rum cocktails

BEACHCOMBER

- *125 ml (4 fl oz) light rum*
- *15 ml ('/₂ fl oz) lemon juice*
- *15 ml ('/₂ fl oz) maraschino liqueur*

Mix the ingredients with shaved ice in a blender. Pour unstrained into a chilled Champagne flute.

BLUE HAWAIIAN

- *50 ml (2 fl oz) white rum*
- *30 ml (1 fl oz) blue curaçao*
- *30 ml (1 fl oz) pineapple juice*
- *5 ml (1 tsp) coconut cream*
- *5 ml (1 tsp) double cream*

Shake ingredients with ice and strain into a chilled cocktail glass to make this lurid blue libation.

CARMEN MIRANDA

- *125 ml (4 fl oz) white rum*
- *30 ml (1 fl oz) lime juice*
- *15 ml ('/₂ oz) Triple Sec*
- *2 dashes of grenadine*

Shake with crushed ice and strain into a chilled cocktail glass. To enter into the spirit of things you can tart this one up with as much fruit as you like. If you substitute the lime juice for lemon juice, it's called a Morning Rose.

CUBA LIBRE

- *50 ml (2 fl oz) light rum*
- *Juice of '/₂ lime*
- *150 ml (5 fl oz) cola*
- *Slice of lime*

No rum section would be complete without the recipe for one of the simplest yet most delicious of drinks.

Pour the rum and lime juice over ice in a Highball glass and stir. Splash in the cola and decorate with the lime slice.

DAIQUIRI

- **40 ml (1¹/₂ fl oz) light rum**
- **Juice of ¹/₂ lime**
- **2.5 ml (¹/₂ tsp) of sugar**

Daiquiri is named after a rum-producing town in Cuba. This is the original recipe for a classic cocktail that today forms the base for numerous fruity and frozen variations. Shake the ingredients vigorously with crushed ice and strain into a chilled cocktail glass. If vermouth and a dash of grenadine are used instead of lime juice, the result is a cocktail called El Presidente.

You can use virtually any fruit you want to make a fruit Daiquiri. Simply pour the ingredients (as above) into a blender with the addition of 40 ml (1¹/₂ fluid ounces) of orange juice, approximately 50 ml (2 fluid ounces) of your chosen fruit and 30 ml (1 fluid ounce) of the corresponding fruit liqueur. Whichever fruit you choose, remember to make sure all skin or peel is removed or your otherwise delicious Daiquiri will take on a rather bitter taste. Highly recommended is a Banana Daiquiri using a crème de bananes liqueur, preferably Bandana from Havana.

To make a frozen Daiquiri, put five or six cracked ice cubes into the blender with the other ingredients and blend for a couple of minutes, or until it has the texture of fine snow. Obviously, fruit and frozen Daiquiris will require larger glasses than the original Daiquiri. I would recommend either a Highball or Collins glass decorated with the appropriate fruit.

GOLDEN GATE

- **50 ml (2 fl oz) dark rum**
- **30 ml (1 fl oz) gin**
- **15 ml (¹/₂ fl oz) crème de cacao**
- **15 ml (¹/₂ fl oz) lemon juice**
- **Pinch of ginger**
- **Slice of orange**

This one should warm your cockles. Shake ingredients with ice and serve on the rocks in an Old-fashioned glass. Decorate with the slice of orange.

HAVANA CLUB

- **85 ml (3 fl oz) Havana Club Golden Rum**
- **30 ml (1 fl oz) dry vermouth**
- **Dash of Angostura bitters**
- **Maraschino cherry**

Stir the ingredients with ice cubes. Serve in a Highball, decorated with a cherry.

KNICKERBOCKER

- *125 ml (4 fl oz) light rum*
- *15 ml ('/2 fl oz) Cointreau*
- *10 ml (2 tsp) orange juice*
- *5 ml (1 tsp) lemon juice*
- *5 ml (1 tsp) pineapple juice*
- *5 ml (1 tsp) raspberry syrup*
- *Pineapple slice*
- *Maraschino cherry*

A very pleasurable way to boost your fruit intake. Shake vigorously with crushed ice and strain into a chilled cocktail glass. Finish by decorating with the pineapple slice and cherry.

LIMEY

- *40 ml (1'/2 fl oz) light rum*
- *25 ml (1'/2 Tbsp) lime liqueur (the Spanish Crema de Lima if you can find any)*
- *10 ml (2 tsp) lime juice*
- *10 ml (2 tsp) Triple Sec*
- *Slice of lime*

Combine ingredients with 125 ml (4 fluid ounces) of crushed ice in a blender. Strain into a Champagne saucer, decorated with the slice of lime.

MAI TAI

- *Juice of 1 lime*
- *20 ml (²/3 fl oz) gold rum*
- *20 ml (²/3 fl oz) dark rum*
- *10 ml ('/3 fl oz) orange curaçao*
- *Dash of orgeat (almond syrup)*
- *Dash of Angostura bitters*
- *Twist of lime peel*
- *Pineapple pieces*
- *Fresh mint*

Fast becoming a modern classic, the Mai Tai tastes innocent enough but don't let that fool you. Pour the ingredients over some ice in an Old-fashioned or Collins glass and stir, or if you are feeling particularly adventurous, a hollowed-out pineapple. Garnish with lime peel, pineapple pieces and fresh mint.

MOUNT FUJI

- **50 ml (2 fl oz) light rum**
- **50 ml (2 fl oz) applejack**
- **30 ml (1 fl oz) Southern Comfort**
- **25 g (1 oz) sugar**
- **Juice of ½ lime (retaining the scooped-out shell)**
- **30 ml (1 fl oz) 151-proof Demerara rum**

This is no blushing violet. In fact it's quite a good ice-breaker at parties just to be seen holding a Mount Fuji. Blend the ingredients, omitting the 151-proof rum, with plenty of ice and pour into a Highball glass. Float the upturned half shell of lime on the surface and pour the 151-proof rum into it. Ignite it. Drink this volcanic cocktail through a long straw if you value your eyebrows.

PIÑA COLADA

- **50 ml (2 fl oz) light rum**
- **50 ml (2 fl oz) pineapple juice**
- **30 ml (1 fl oz) coconut milk**
- **15 ml (½ fl oz) double cream**
- **1 hollowed-out coconut (strictly optional)**
- **Slice of pineapple**
- **Maraschino cherry**

Combine the ingredients in a blender with ice, being careful to omit the hollowed-out coconut at this stage. The coconut is to drink it out of. If you don't want to look like one of the Flintstones, however, a large goblet or Collins glass will suffice. Decorate with a pineapple slice and maraschino cherry. If you prefer, Piña Coladas can be shaken.

PLANTER'S PUNCH

- *85 ml (3 fl oz) Jamaica rum*
- *30 ml (1 fl oz) lime juice*
- *30 ml (1 fl oz) orange juice*
- *85 ml (3 fl oz) pineapple juice (optional)*
- *Dash of grenadine*
- *2 dashes of Angostura bitters*
- *Slice of lime*

Traditionally made with Myers rum from Jamaica, Planter's Punch is one of the oldest rum-based cocktails. There are countless variations of it, but one of the earliest versions is summed up in an old rhyme: 'One of sour (lime juice), two of sweet (sugar syrup), three of strong (rum), four of weak (ice).'

Shake the ingredients with crushed ice and pour into a Collins glass. Add more ice if desired, stir and decorate with a slice of lime.

ZOMBIE

- *50 ml (2 fl oz) light rum*
- *50 ml (2 fl oz) gold rum*
- *50 ml (2 fl oz) dark rum*
- *30 ml (1 fl oz) apricot brandy*
- *15 ml (¹/₂ fl oz) lime juice*
- *30 ml (1 fl oz) orange juice*
- *50 ml (2 fl oz) pineapple juice*
- *Dash of grenadine*
- *15 ml (¹/₂ fl oz) 151-proof Demerara rum*
- *Slice of orange*
- *Slice of lemon*
- *Sprig of fresh mint*
- *2 cherries (1 red, 1 green)*

One glimpse at the colourful epithet and the ingredients of this drink should be enough to tell you that this is the mother of all rum cocktails. Shake all the ingredients, omitting the Demerara rum, in a mixing glass with ice. Pour into a large glass and float the Demerara rum onto the surface using the back of a teaspoon. Decorate with orange and lemon slices, mint and multicoloured cherries. You might as well bung in a sparkler, an umbrella and a plastic monkey while you're at it. Incidentally, there is such a thing as a special Zombie glass, but a Collins glass is just as effective.

SHERRY

A D O N I S

- 50 ml (2 fl oz) dry sherry
- 30 ml (1 fl oz) sweet vermouth
- 2 dashes of Angostura bitters
- Dash of orange bitters (optional)
- Twist of orange peel

Stir thoroughly in a mixing glass containing three or four ice cubes. Strain into a cocktail glass and decorate with orange peel.

sherry cocktails

CORONATION

- 30 ml (1 fl oz) dry sherry
- 30 ml (1 fl oz) dry vermouth
- 85 ml (3 fl oz) white wine
- 2 dashes of Angostura bitters
- Dash of maraschino liqueur
- Top up with chilled soda

Stir with cracked ice in a mixing glass.
Serve in a Highball glass topped up
with soda.

GRANADA

- 50 ml (2 fl oz) dry sherry
- 50 ml (2 fl oz) brandy
- 30 ml (1 fl oz) orange curaçao
- Top up with chilled tonic water
- Slice of orange

Stir with ice in a mixing glass then pour
into a Highball glass. Top up with tonic
water and decorate with the orange slice.

IMELDA

- 50 ml (2 fl oz) cream sherry
- 30 ml (1 fl oz) kirsch
- 30 ml (1 fl oz) orange juice
- 30 ml (1 fl oz) lemon juice
- Top up with chilled Champagne
- Slice of orange
- Slice of lemon
- Maraschino cherry

Mix all the ingredients except the
Champagne in a blender with three or
four ice cubes. Pour into a large goblet
or Highball glass and top up with
Champagne. Decorate with fruit.
If served in a glass slipper this becomes
an Imelda Marcos.

SHERRY COBBLER

- 5 ml (1 tsp) sugar syrup
- Dash of grenadine
- Dash of orange curaçao
- 85 ml (3 fl oz) medium sherry

Pour the ingredients into a large goblet
over crushed ice. Pour the sugar syrup

first, followed by the grenadine and
curaçao then the sherry. Give it a
thorough stir and decorate with seasonal
fruits, as is the tradition. Excellent
cobblers can also be made with port,
Sauternes, light white wines or claret
in place of the sherry.

TEQUILA

CARABINIERI

- 40 ml (1¹/₂ fl oz) tequila
- 30 ml (1 fl oz) Galliano
- 15 ml (¹/₂ fl oz) Cointreau
- 85 ml (3 fl oz) fresh orange juice
- 5 ml (1 tsp) lime juice
- Yolk of 1 egg
- Slice of lime
- 2 cherries (1 red, 1 green)

Here's a tequila-based fruit cocktail in a glass. The egg yolk and fresh orange juice make it the ideal cocktail if you missed breakfast.

Shake the ingredients vigorously and strain into a Collins glass over crushed ice. Spruce it up with the slice of lime and cherries.

IMAGINATION

- 30 ml (1 fl oz) tequila
- 50 ml (2 fl oz) orange curaçao
- 50 ml (2 fl oz) coconut milk
- 50 ml (2 fl oz) double cream

Firstly, I'd like to apologise for the appalling name of this cream cocktail. You might never be able to bring yourself to ask for an *Imagination* in a crowded bar, but at least now you'll be able to make one in the privacy of your own home. And what you get up to in your own time is your business, right?

Shake thoroughly with ice and strain into a large cocktail glass with crushed ice.

MARGARITA

- *Wedge of lime*
- *Coarse salt*
- *85 ml (3 fl oz) golden tequila*
- *30 ml (1 fl oz) Triple Sec*
- *50–85 ml (2–3 fl oz) lime juice*
- *Slice of lime*

What beats an ice-cold Margarita with friends after a helluva day? Nothing. The Margarita is a deliciously refreshing modern classic with a tangy, sophisticated flavour all its own.

Frost the rim of a chilled cocktail glass by running a wedge of lime around the rim and twisting the upturned glass in a shallow dish of coarse salt. Shake the remaining ingredients in an ice-filled shaker and strain into your salt-edged glass. Decorate with a slice of lime. Simplicity itself.

You could use clear tequila, known as white or silver tequila, but golden tequila, which takes its warm hue from at least three years' maturation in oak casks, will deliver a smoother, fuller flavour. If in doubt, remember the cocktail code: best use the best for the best.

To make a frosted Margarita, pulverize in a blender the tequila, Triple Sec and lime juice with cracked ice.

MAYAN WHORE

- *40 ml (1¹/₂ fl oz) tequila*
- *85 ml (3 fl oz) chilled pineapple juice*
- *Chilled soda*
- *30 ml (1 fl oz) Kahlúa*

It's time to get out your spirit level to make this layered cocktail. For that crazy stripy effect, first pour the tequila into a tallish straight-sided glass followed by the pineapple juice. Next, pour in some soda and then float the Kahlúa on top. Allow the layers to settle and then sip it sedately through a straw. I appreciate that the name of this cocktail is in rather poor taste but it has to be said that it slides down like a whore's drawers.

TEQUILA SHOTS

- *1 fridge of tequila*
- *1 large bag of salt*
- *1 sack of limes*
- *1 kitchen of party animals*
- *1 table*
- *1 recording of Motorhead's* Ace of Spades *(optional)*
- *Positively no decoration*

Pour a generous tequila shot for each participant and pour a small amount of salt on to the backs of their hands. Ask casually what the time is. Replace the salt for the morons in your party. Give each person a wedge of lime. When Lemmy says 'I don't want to live for ever', lick the salt off the back of your hand, slam your glasses on the table, knock back the chilled tequila in one, and suck on the lime wedge.

TEQUILA SUNRISE

- *50 ml (2 fl oz) tequila*
- *125 ml (4 fl oz) fresh orange juice*
- *30 ml (1 fl oz) grenadine*
- *Slice of orange*
- *Maraschino cherry*

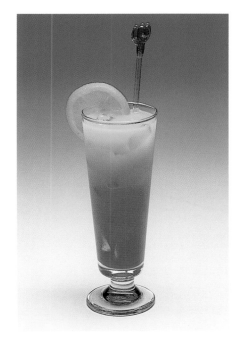

After the exertions of the Tequila Shots ritual (see above), you might like to slip on the best of the Eagles before drifting into a Tequila Sunrise. Pour the tequila over ice in a Highball glass. Add the orange juice then drop the grenadine into the centre of the drink. The grenadine will gradually sink to the bottom. Decorate with a slice of orange and a cherry.

An alternative version, named the Tequila Sunset, is made with golden tequila, lemon juice and clear honey.

VERMOUTH

ALFONSO

- *2.5 ml ('/₂ tsp) sugar*
- *50 ml (2 fl oz) sweet vermouth*
- *2 dashes of Angostura bitters*
- *Top up with chilled Champagne*
- *Twist of lemon peel*

Put three or four lumps of ice in a Highball glass and sprinkle on the sugar. Pour in the vermouth, add the Angostura bitters and stir it well. Top up with Champagne and decorate with a twist of lemon.

vermouth cocktails

AMERICAN BEAUTY

- 50 ml (2 fl oz) dry vermouth
- 15 ml (¹/₂ fl oz) white crème de menthe
- 50 ml (2 fl oz) orange juice
- 50 ml (2 fl oz) brandy
- Dash of grenadine
- 5 ml (1 tsp) port

Shake all the ingredients, except the port, with some crushed ice. Strain into a large chilled cocktail glass. Float the port on top.

THE CLARIDGE

- 30 ml (1 fl oz) dry vermouth
- 30 ml (1 fl oz) London dry gin
- 15 ml (¹/₂ fl oz) Cointreau
- 15 ml (¹/₂ fl oz) apricot brandy

Gracious living in a glass and an excellent apéritif to boot. Shake with ice cubes and strain into a cocktail glass. This recipe comes from *The Savoy Cocktail Book*.

DIABLO

- 40 ml (1¹/₂ fl oz) dry white port
- 30 ml (1 fl oz) sweet vermouth
- Dash of lemon juice

Shake ingredients with ice and strain into a chilled cocktail glass.
  The Devil's Cocktail is a similarly demonic drink. Following the same process, use red port and dry vermouth instead.

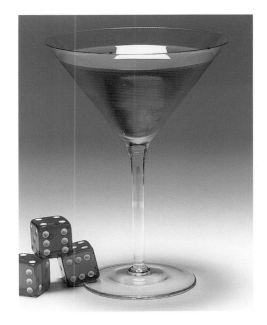

SOUL KISS

- 30 ml (1 fl oz) dry vermouth
- 50 ml (2 fl oz) bourbon
- 30 ml (1 fl oz) orange juice
- 5 ml (1 tsp) Dubonnet

Shake with cracked ice and strain into a chilled cocktail glass. Replacing the orange juice and Dubonnet with a dash of orange bitters and a dash of grenadine makes a Trocadero.

VODKA

BIKINI

- *85 ml (3 fl oz) vodka*
- *30 ml (1 fl oz) white rum*
- *Juice of ¹/₂ lemon*
- *15 ml (¹/₂ fl oz) milk*
- *5 ml (1 tsp) sugar*

Shake ingredients with cracked ice. Strain into a chilled cocktail glass.

BLACK RUSSIAN

- *85 ml (3 fl oz) vodka*
- *30 ml (1 fl oz) Kahlúa*
- *Top up with chilled cola (optional)*

Pour vodka and Kahlúa over ice in a Highball glass or Champagne flute and stir. Top up with cola, if you wish, for a taller Black Russian.

BLOODY MARY

- *85 ml (3 fl oz) vodka*
- *125 ml (4 fl oz) tomato juice (or more, to taste)*
- *15 ml ('/2 fl oz) lemon juice (optional)*
- *15 ml ('/2 fl oz) lime juice (optional)*
- *Dash of Worcestershire sauce (optional)*
- *Salt and pepper (optional)*
- *2 drops of Tabasco sauce (optional)*
- *Celery stick (optional)*
- *Slice of cucumber (optional)*
- *Slice of lemon (optional)*

Bloody Mary is the cocktail mixer's minefield. Every man and his dog knows the perfect recipe, so be ready for plenty of backseat mixing. About the only agreement you'll find concerning the Bloody Mary is that it contains vodka and tomato juice. So, to make the most basic Bloody Mary of them all, shake vodka and tomato juice with ice and serve in a Highball glass. You will find on reflection, however, that this is not the most exciting of cocktails. To give it real spicy pizzazz, I strongly recommend the addition of all the above extras to the strongest degree your tastebuds can handle. In my opinion, the perfect Bloody Mary is hotter than hell with a helluva kick. Garnish the finished cocktail as you see fit, using any combination of celery sticks and slices of cucumber and lemon.

You might like to decorate the rim of your glass with celery salt before you start. (See Margarita recipe on page 50.)

The omission of vodka leaves a non-alcoholic though still pretty punchy little number known as a Virgin Mary.

Going to the other extreme, replace half the tomato juice with condensed beef stock, spike it with a little extra hot chilli and call it a Bloodshot. A Bullshot omits the tomato juice. A cocktail made with just the lemon juice and Worcestershire sauce is called Bullshit.

BLUE LAGOON

- *50 ml (2 fl oz) vodka*
- *40 ml (1¹/₂ fl oz) blue curaçao*
- *15 ml (¹/₂ fl oz) lemon juice*
- *Top up with chilled soda*
- *Blue cocktail cherry*

I've included this one only so that
you can have the opportunity to
pose with a blue vodka.

Pour the vodka and blue curaçao
over ice in a large goblet. Add
lemon juice, top up with soda and
stir. Spike a blue cherry with a blue
plastic cocktail stick. Marvel at the
blueness of it.

COSMOPOLITAN

- *50 ml (2 fl oz) vodka (lemon-flavoured)*
- *15 ml (¹/₂ fl oz) Triple Sec*
- *30 ml (1 fl oz) cranberry juice*
- *Dash of fresh lime juice*
- *Orange zest*

The Cosmopolitan is fiendishly trendy.
Give the ingredients a thorough shaking
with some ice then pour through a
strainer into a chilled cocktail glass.

FRESH FRUITINI

- *50 ml (2 fl oz) vodka*
- *Some fresh fruit of any kind, sliced*
- *Dash of sugar syrup*
- *2 dashes of orange bitters (optional)*

This style of Martini is very popular
at present and is one of the freshest-
tasting drinks you could ever create.
It's desperately simple to make and any
type of fresh fruit can be used, though
pineapple and strawberry come highly
recommended.

Force the sliced fruit through a fine sieve
with the back of a spoon into a shaker.
Pour in the vodka and sugar syrup and
shake vigorously with ice. Strain into a
chilled cocktail glass decorated with the
appropriate fruit.

vodka cocktails

GOLDEN TANG

- *125 ml (4 fl oz) vodka*
- *50 ml (2 fl oz) Strega (Italian fruit and herb liqueur)*
- *30 ml (1 fl oz) orange juice*
- *30 ml (1 fl oz) crème de banane*

Shake the ingredients with ice and serve in a Highball glass.

GRAND DUCHESS

- *85 ml (3 fl oz) vodka*
- *40 ml (1¹/₂ fl oz) dark rum*
- *40 ml (1¹/₂ fl oz) lime juice*
- *25 ml (³/₄ fl oz) grenadine*

This one reminds me of an old boss of mine. Shake ingredients with cracked ice and strain into a chilled cocktail glass.

GREEN DEMON

- *40 ml (1¹/₂ fl oz) vodka*
- *30 ml (1 fl oz) light rum*
- *30 ml (1 fl oz) melon liqueur*
- *Top up with chilled lemonade (to taste)*
- *Small slice of watermelon*
- *Green cocktail cherry*

Shake all ingredients, except the lemonade, with cracked ice. Serve in a large goblet, topped up with lemonade and decorated with the unusual combination of watermelon and a green cherry.

HARVEY WALLBANGER

- *40 ml (1¹/₂ fl oz) vodka*
- *30 ml (1 fl oz) Galliano*
- *Top up with chilled orange juice (to taste)*
- *Slice of lemon*

Pour the vodka and Galliano over ice in a Highball glass. Top up with freshly squeezed orange juice and decorate with a lemon slice.

Stories abound concerning how this cocktail earned its ridiculous name, the most plausible of which concerns a six-foot tall, invisible, white rabbit.

Replacing vodka with tequila makes a Freddy Fudpucker.

KANGAROO

- *85 ml (3 fl oz) vodka*
- *40 ml (1¹/₂ fl oz) dry vermouth*
- *Twist of lemon peel*

Stir ingredients with crushed ice and strain into a chilled cocktail glass. Decorate with lemon peel.

KATINKA

- *50 ml (2 fl oz) vodka*
- *40 ml (1¹/₂ fl oz) apricot brandy*
- *15 ml (¹/₂ fl oz) lime juice*
- *Fresh mint*

Shake ingredients thoroughly and serve over crushed ice in a cocktail glass. Decorate with mint.

LONG ISLAND ICED TEA

- *30 ml (1 fl oz) vodka*
- *30 ml (1 fl oz) gin*
- *30 ml (1 fl oz) tequila*
- *30 ml (1 fl oz) light rum*
- *85 ml (3 fl oz) chilled cola*
- *30 ml (1 fl oz) lime juice*
- *15 ml (¹/₂ fl oz) Cointreau*
- *5 ml (1 tsp) sugar syrup (optional)*
- *Slice of lemon*
- *Fresh mint leaves (optional)*

As you can see, the Long Island Iced Tea could have appeared just as happily in the gin, tequila or rum sections of this book. It's the perfect cocktail for indecisive drinkers and might explain why it is so widely popular. Or maybe it doesn't. Pour the ingredients over ice in a Highball glass. Stir briskly and decorate with the lemon slice and fresh mint.

MOSCOW MULE

- *50 ml (2 fl oz) vodka*
- *30 ml (1 fl oz) lime juice*
- *Top with chilled ginger beer or dry ginger ale*
- *Slice of lime*

The Moscow Mule is awesomely trendy, but that's no bad thing given it tastes so good. It's not as if it contains Kümmel or Parfait Amour, for example.

Stir the vodka and lime juice in a Highball glass half-filled with ice. Top up with ginger beer or dry ginger ale. Decorate with a slice of lime.

NINITCHKA

- *85 ml (3 fl oz) vodka*
- *50 ml (2 fl oz) crème de cacao*
- *30 ml (1 fl oz) lemon juice*

Shake with cracked ice and strain into a chilled cocktail glass. If you add a couple of dashes of grenadine—something I try to avoid whenever possible—you will end up with another suitably Russian-sounding cocktail, the Kretchma.

ROAD RUNNER

- *50 ml (2 fl oz) vodka*
- *30 ml (1 fl oz) amaretto*
- *30 ml (1 fl oz) coconut milk*
- *Pinch of grated nutmeg*

Meep! Meep! Pour the ingredients into a shaker with cracked ice and shake as hard as you can. Strain into a cocktail glass and sprinkle with nutmeg. Raise your glass to victimized coyotes everywhere.

SALTY DOG

- *Wedge of lemon*
- *Coarse salt*
- *50 ml (2 fl oz) vodka*
- *Top up with chilled fresh grapefruit juice (to taste)*

This is vodka's answer to the Margarita. Vodka is often the answer to everything since it is so versatile. I totally dispute the misguided notion that vodka is tasteless. It always tastes to me surprisingly like vodka, in the same way that gin has the uncanny habit of tasting like gin. But I suppose if you're the kind of person who believes that black and white aren't colours you'll also think that vodka is the one and only substance in the whole of creation that tastes of precisely nothing. Some feat.

Frost the rim of a Highball glass using lemon juice and coarse salt (see the Margarita recipe on page 50). Half-fill the glass with ice cubes and pour over the vodka. Top up with grapefruit juice to taste. Throw in the lemon wedge to give the grapefruit juice just a bit more edge.

SEA BREEZE

- *50 ml (2 fl oz) vodka*
- *Top up with equal measures of cranberry and grapefruit juice (I prefer a heftier dose of cranberry juice)*
- *Slice of orange*

This could be even trendier than the Moscow Mule. It certainly tastes as good so no one's complaining. The sweetness of the cranberry juice works wonderfully with the tartness of the grapefruit juice, punctuated by a kick of vodka. It adds up to a sunny day at the seaside in a glass and proves beyond question that cocktails do not need to be complicated to be orgasmic.

Pour the vodka over ice in a Highball glass. Top up with chilled cranberry and grapefruit juice. Stir, decorate with a sunny slice of orange, sit back and listen to the seagulls.

Incidentally, vodka, cranberry juice and peach schnapps instead of grapefruit juice makes the not-stupidly-named-at-all Woo Woo.

vodka cocktails

VOLGA BOATMAN

- *85 ml (3 fl oz) vodka*
- *30 ml (1 fl oz) kirsch*
- *30 ml (1 fl oz) orange juice*

Shake with cracked ice and strain into a chilled cocktail glass. This is named after Europe's longest river, the mighty Volga (3,689 km/2,293 miles), which rises in the Valdai mountain range in western Russia and flows into the Caspian Sea in the south via the port of Volgograd. It is *not* named after a Russian sailor who was obsessed by how much money the rest of the crew were earning.

WHITE RUSSIAN

- *50 ml (2 fl oz) vodka*
- *30 ml (1 fl oz) Kahlúa*
- *50 ml (2 fl oz) double cream*
- *Grated nutmeg and grated chocolate*

If you really believe vodka doesn't taste of anything and that black and white aren't real colours (see Salty Dog recipe, opposite), don't waste your time with either a Black or White Russian.

Shake the ingredients with ice until you can barely see straight. Then pour into a Highball glass and serve with a sprinkling of grated nutmeg and grated chocolate on the top. It's creamy and dreamy.

WHISKY

BARBARY COAST

- *50 ml (2 fl oz) Scotch*
- *30 ml (1 fl oz) gin*
- *30 ml (1 fl oz) crème de cacao*
- *30 ml (1 fl oz) double cream*
- *Grated nutmeg or grated chocolate*

A cream cocktail to kick off our whisky section. Shake with cracked ice and strain into a chilled cocktail glass. Decorate with either a pinch of nutmeg or grated chocolate.

BROOKLYN

- *85 ml (3 fl oz) bourbon*
- *30 ml (1 fl oz) dry vermouth*
- *Dash of Amer Picon (a bitter French liqueur)*
- *Dash of maraschino liqueur*

Allegedly first dreamed up at the St George Hotel in Brooklyn, this cocktail, through the addition of maraschino liqueur, is a slightly sweeter version of its more self-assured big brother, the Manhattan. Can be shaken or stirred with cracked ice. Serve in a chilled cocktail glass.

BOURBON COCKTAIL

- *50 ml (2 fl oz) bourbon*
- *15 ml ('/2 fl oz) orange curaçao*
- *15 ml ('/2 fl oz) Benedictine*
- *30 ml (1 fl oz) lemon juice*
- *Dash of Angostura bitters*
- *Slice of orange (optional)*

Shake ingredients thoroughly with cracked ice and strain into a chilled cocktail glass. Decorate with a slice of orange.

CANADIAN COCKTAIL

- *50 ml (2 fl oz) bourbon*
- *2 dashes of orange curaçao*
- *Dash of Angostura bitters*
- *2.5 ml ('/2 tsp) sugar syrup (or to taste)*
- *Twist of lemon*

Shake ingredients with cracked ice. Strain into a cocktail glass and zap it with a twist of lemon (squeeze a thin slice of peel, skin-side down over the surface). Nonchalantly drop the peel in if you like. Yes, it's amazing isn't it? The Canadian

Cocktail does not contain any Canadian whisky. In truth, Canadian whisky is a bit of a wallflower sitting by the dance-floor of the Cocktail Club. The more gregarious mixers can ask it to dance but tend to drown its lightness of body and flavour. Though perhaps, with tastes generally shifting towards lighter styles, Canadian whisky might learn a few new steps. But all is not lost, here's how to make a Carlton Cocktail.

CARLTON COCKTAIL

- **50 ml (2 fl oz) Canadian whisky**
- **30 ml (1 fl oz) orange curaçao**
- **30 ml (1 fl oz) fresh orange juice**
- **Slice of lemon (optional)**

Shake ingredients with cracked ice and strain into a chilled cocktail glass. Top with a slice of lemon.

FLYING SCOTSMAN

- **50 ml (2 fl oz) Scotch**
- **50 ml (2 fl oz) sweet vermouth**
- **Dash of Angostura bitters**
- **Dash of sugar syrup (or to taste)**

This is sweetened up Scotch for those who might otherwise find Scotch whisky too, shall we say, robust.

Give ingredients a thorough stir with ice and strain into a chilled cocktail glass.

FRISCO

- **50 ml (2 fl oz) bourbon**
- **15 ml (¹/₂ fl oz) Benedictine**
- **Twist of lemon**

From the beautiful city by the bay comes the frisky Frisco. Stir the ingredients with cracked ice and strain into a chilled cocktail glass. Decorate with a lemon twist.

Benedictine is made to a secret recipe of herbs and spices, rumoured to be based on brandy. It was developed about 1510 at the Benedictine monastery at Fécamp in northern France, a place worth visiting. Its architectural style of Disneyland meets the Addams family is pure gothic fantasy. Curiously, the liqueur was very popular in working-men's clubs in Lancashire, as a consequence of soldiers from these parts being stationed at Fécamp in the First World War.

GLOOM LIFTER

- **50 ml (2 fl oz) Irish whisky**
- **15 ml (¹/₂ fl oz) lemon juice**
- **5 ml (1 tsp) sugar syrup**
- **1 egg white**
- **5 ml (1 tsp) brandy (optional)**
- **Dash of grenadine (optional)**
- **Dash of framboise (raspberry syrup) (optional)**

At last, an opportunity to play with Irish whisky. Shake with cracked ice and strain into a large, chilled cocktail glass.

HORSE'S NECK (WITH A KICK)

- *85 ml (3 fl oz) bourbon, or rye, or Scotch or Irish*
- *1 lemon*
- *Top up with chilled ginger ale*

It's unusual to find a cocktail that seems to have been named after the decoration used in a soft drink. The original version, the Horse's Neck, is a refreshing, alcohol-free, summer drink. To make one of these, peel a whole lemon in an unbroken spiral (this might take a few attempts) and hang it over the side of a Collins glass, with most of it *inside* the glass. Presumably, this is like hanging something around a horse's neck? Drop in some ice cubes and top it up with fizzing ginger ale.

To make a Horse's Neck (with a Kick), just pour in the whisky before the ginger ale. Gin, rum or applejack can be used, but the best marriage with ginger ale, in my opinion, is whisky.

IRISH COCKTAIL

- *50 ml (2 fl oz) Irish whisky*
- *6 dashes of crème de menthe*
- *3 dashes of green Chartreuse*
- *2 cherries (1 green, 1 red)*

Appropriately, this cocktail is emerald green. It's also cool, minty and delicious. Shake ingredients and strain into a chilled cocktail glass. Decorate with the red and green cherries.

LADIES' COCKTAIL

- *50 ml (2 fl oz) bourbon*
- *5 ml (1 tsp) Pernod*
- *2.5 ml (¹/₂ tsp) anisette*
- *3 dashes of Angostura bitters*
- *Slice of pineapple*

As Barry White would say, this one's for all the ladies. Stir ingredients in a mixing glass with some cracked ice cubes. Strain into a chilled cocktail glass and decorate with pineapple.

MANHATTAN

- **85 ml (3 fl oz) rye or bourbon**
- **40 ml (1¹/₂ fl oz) sweet vermouth**
- **2 dashes of Angostura bitters**
- **Maraschino cherry**

As with the Dry Martini (see page 28), connoisseurs get very worked up over what is the 'correct' Manhattan recipe. Did you know that more New Yorkers are murdered each year while arguing about these two cocktails than are murdered while discussing *all* other cocktails combined? Rye whisky is more commonly used than bourbon to make Manhattans, but you're the one who's going to drink it so you decide which tastes better.

Give the ingredients a thorough stir with ice cubes in a mixing glass and strain into a chilled cocktail glass. Decorate with a maraschino cherry. There, that wasn't too complicated was it?

For a Dry Manhattan swap sweet for dry vermouth, and maybe a twist of lemon in place of the cherry. Some prefer an olive with their Dry Manhattans, but I'm not convinced.

A French-style Manhattan uses dry vermouth and adds a dash of Cointreau.

If you happen to prefer your Manhattans made with Scotch whisky you can come out of the closet now. It's okay if you call it a Rob Roy. You're also allowed to add a couple of teaspoonfuls of lime juice and a few dashes of orange curaçao to a basic Manhattan, but only if you call it a Grand Slam. Please take these simple precautions or the cocktail police will get you.

MILLIONAIRE

- *5 ml (1 tsp) grenadine*
- *5 ml (1 tsp) framboise (raspberry syrup)*
- *30 ml (1 fl oz) orange curaçao*
- *1 egg white*
- *85 ml (3 fl oz) rye, bourbon, Scotch or Irish*

Shake the grenadine, framboise, curaçao and egg white with cracked ice. Add the whisky and shake again. Serve in a chilled cocktail glass.

MINT JULEP

- *5 ml (1 tsp) sugar syrup*
- *6 fresh mint leaves (young, small and tender)*
- *Dash of Angostura bitters (optional)*
- *85 ml (3 fl oz) bourbon*
- *Plenty of crushed ice*
- *5 ml (1 tsp) icing sugar*
- *Paper napkin*
- *Drinking straws*
- *5 ml (1 tsp) of bourbon or rum (optional)*

The Mint Julep is a very tall and refreshing drink so, depending on how tall and refreshing you want it, use either a Collins or a Highball glass. Whichever you go for, it's a good idea to chill your glass first.

Put the sugar syrup and three mint leaves in a mixing glass with an optional dash of Angostura bitters. Gently bruise the mint leaves with the back of a bar spoon. Do not pulverize them as this can

release an unwanted bitter flavour. Pour in the bourbon and give it another gentle stir.

Nearly fill your chosen glass with very finely crushed ice. Remember Archimedes' principle, so do leave a little space for your minty mixture. Give it a good stir.

To decorate, rinse your three remaining mint leaves and dip them in icing sugar. Clip the ends of the stems to allow the slow release of mint juices into your cocktail.

The paper napkin allows you to pick up your Mint Julep and put the drinking straws to your mouth without warming the glass with your hands.

It isn't over yet. Some people like to float 5 ml (1 teaspoon) of bourbon or rum on to the top of their Juleps. This is not punishable by death as others might tell you. One of the first written recordings of the Mint Julep was by an Englishman, Captain Maryatt, who, in 1815, visited a wealthy planter in America's Deep South. He was served the prototype Mint Juleps which were based on—shock horror!—brandy, peach brandy, claret or Madeira. It was only with the outbreak of the Civil War that the use of bourbon became both expedient and patriotic.

Incidentally, the word *Julep* comes from a Persian word *gulab*, meaning a pleasant-tasting drink similar to rose water in which vile medicines could be disguised.

OLD-FASHIONED

- *5 ml (1 tsp) sugar syrup*
- *2 dashes of Angostura bitters*
- *85 ml (3 fl oz) rye or bourbon*
- *Dash of orange curaçao (optional)*
- *Top up with chilled soda (optional)*
- *Twist of lemon*
- *Twist of orange*
- *Maraschino cherry (optional)*

Another cocktail to have caused otherwise sane individuals to attack each other in bars with soda syphons and ice buckets. It's all very unnecessary really. This classic cocktail has its very own glass named after it, so surely it's self-assured enough to allow a little interpretation?

The key to this one is in the stirring. Thus the Old-fashioned provides an alternative way to develop strong wrists. Pour the sugar syrup and Angostura into an Old-fashioned glass. Muddle them together with a bar spoon, add 30 ml (1 fluid ounce) of the whisky and stir again. Add two or three large cracked ice cubes and stir again. Pour over the remaining whisky. Stir it even more. For some, the odd dash or two of orange curaçao will improve this cocktail. You could really upset some purists by adding a touch of soda. Decorate with any combination of the orange and lemon, and maybe lob in a maraschino cherry.

RATTLESNAKE

- *50 ml (2 fl oz) rye*
- *15 ml (¹/₂ fl oz) Pernod*
- *Juice of ¹/₂ lemon*
- *2.5 ml (¹/₂ tsp) icing sugar*
- *1 egg white*

Shake with cracked ice until it is quite frothy then strain into a chilled cocktail glass. This has quite a bite, courtesy of the Pernod and lemon juice.

RUSTY NAIL

- *50 ml (2 fl oz) Scotch*
- *30 ml (1 fl oz) Drambuie*
- *Twist of lemon*

The natural partnership of Scotch whisky and Drambuie liqueur is popular with whisky drinkers the world over. Pour the Scotch then the Drambuie into an Old-fashioned glass. Add some cubed ice and decorate the drink with a lemon twist. The same mixture can be stirred in a mixing glass and served over crushed ice in a Highball glass.

Drambuie is a blend of Scotch whisky, heather honey, herbs and spices. It dates

from 1745 and its name comes from the Gaelic *an dram buidheach*, meaning 'the drink that satisfies'.

SCOTCH SOLACE

- *85 ml (3 fl oz) Scotch*
- *30 ml (1 fl oz) Triple Sec*
- *5 ml (1 tsp) clear honey*
- *50 ml (2 fl oz) double cream*
- *Top up with milk (to taste)*
- *Pinch of grated nutmeg (optional)*
- *Twist of orange or lemon (optional)*

Here's one of the few recipes to partner whisky with cream. Is this why it's called a Scotch Solace? Pour the Scotch and Triple Sec into an ice-filled Highball glass. Stir in the honey then add the cream and milk. Put some spring into its step with some grated nutmeg or a twist of orange or lemon.

This recipe is, of course, a distant relative of the Hot Toddy which gives great solace to cold symptoms. Pour 40 ml (1¹/₂ fluid ounces) of Scotch and 15 ml (¹/₂ fluid ounce) of lemon juice into an Old-fashioned glass. Top up with boiling water and add 5 ml (1 teaspoon) of sugar, two cloves and a generous pinch of ground cinnamon.

WARD EIGHT

- *50 ml (2 fl oz) bourbon*
- *30 ml (1 fl oz) lemon juice*
- *30 ml (1 fl oz) orange juice*
- *Dash of grenadine*

Shake with cracked ice and strain into a chilled cocktail glass. Alternatively, this makes a delicious long drink when served over masses of finely crushed ice in a Highball glass.

WHISKY SOUR

- *85 ml (3 fl oz) Scotch, Irish, rye or bourbon (only one of these, not all of them)*
- *25 ml (³/₄ fl oz) lemon juice*
- *8 ml (¹/₄ fl oz) sugar syrup (or to taste)*
- *2 dashes of Angostura bitters (optional)*
- *Twist of lemon peel*

The original Sour Puss. Shake ingredients with cracked ice and strain into an Old-fashioned glass or, indeed, a cocktail glass. Zap it with the lemon twist. Please remember that fresh lemon juice makes all the difference.

WINE

OPERATOR

- **Dry white wine**
- **5 ml (1 tsp) lime juice**
- **Top up with chilled ginger ale**
- **Slice of lemon or lime**

Instant summer refreshment, and a bit more interesting than a straight Spritzer. Pour white wine over some ice cubes in a Highball glass. Add lime juice and top up with ginger ale. Decorate with a slice of lemon or lime.

wine cocktails

SANGRIA

- 1 bottle of dry red wine, preferably Spanish
- 85 ml (3 fl oz) brandy
- 50 ml (2 fl oz) orange curaçao
- 85 ml (3 fl oz) orange juice
- 85 ml (3 fl oz) lemon juice
- 10 ml (2 tsp) icing sugar
- Top up with chilled soda (optional)
- ½ orange, finely sliced
- ½ apple, finely sliced

This version of the Spanish wine spectacular serves four. Stir all ingredients, except the soda, with lots of ice in a large jug. You might like to top this up with soda, depending on how much ice you've used. Decorate with sliced fruit.

WHITE WINE COOLER

- 150 ml (5 fl oz) dry white wine
- 30 ml (1 fl oz) brandy
- 2.5 ml (½ tsp) sugar syrup (optional)
- Dash of Angostura bitters
- Dash of Kümmel
- Top up with chilled soda
- Twist of cucumber peel

Shake ingredients with cracked ice and serve in a Highball glass or large goblet. Top up with soda. Decorate with cucumber.

71

OTHER SPIRITS

APPLEJACK FIZZ

- *85 ml (3 fl oz) applejack (calvados)*
- *Juice of ¹/₂ lemon*
- *5 ml (1 tsp) sugar syrup*
- *Slice of orange*
- *Maraschino cherry*

Depending on where you come from, this cocktail is known as an Applejack Fizz or a Calvados Sour.

Shake ingredients with ice and strain into a small, straight-sided tumbler. Decorate with orange and a cherry.

A Q U A V I T   C L A M

- **85 ml (3 fl oz) aquavit**
- **50 ml (2 fl oz) clam juice and 50 ml (2 fl oz) tomato juice (or 125 ml (4 fl oz) Clamato juice)**
- **5 ml (1 tsp) lemon juice**
- **Worcestershire sauce, salt and Tabasco sauce, to taste**

Aquavit hails from Scandinavia where it is distilled from grain or potatoes. Its main flavouring agent is caraway seed. Usually it is drunk ice-cold, by the shot from chilled glasses. To you, this recipe might sound a bit like a fishy Bloody Mary. But trust me.

Stir ingredients in a mixing glass. Serve in a Highball glass with plenty of ice.

C A I P I R I N H A

- **125 ml (4 fl oz) cachaca**
- **1 lime**
- **10 ml (2 tsp) sugar**

From Scandinavia to South America. Cachaca (pronounced ka-sha-sa) is a clear sugar cane spirit from Brazil. So, to all intents and purposes, it is a form of rum. The Caipirinha, the most popular use for cachaca, tastes very pleasantly of sweetened limes, but take a look at those proportions. I enjoyed a couple of Caipirinhas in a bar in Madrid and, afterwards, could just as well have been in downtown Rio. In this drink, the role of lime is extended way beyond that of a mere decoration. It plays an integral part.

Slice the lime into eight pieces and put them in a sturdy tumbler. Add the sugar and crush with a pestle. Pour in the cachaca and add some ice cubes. I urge you to try this.

P I M M S

- *50 ml (2 fl oz) Pimms No. 1 (gin-based)*
- *Top up with chilled lemonade, soda or ginger ale*
- *Slice of lemon*
- *Slice of orange*
- *Cucumber peel*
- *Sprig of mint*

This drink could be a Merchant Ivory production. Now available in cans.

Pour Pimms No. 1 over ice in a Highball glass. Top up with lemonade, soda or ginger ale. Decorate with the slices of fruit, cucumber peel and fresh mint.

P I S C O   S O U R

- *5 ml (1 tsp) sugar syrup or icing sugar*
- *30 ml (1 fl oz) lemon juice*
- *125 ml (4 fl oz) Pisco*
- *Slice of lemon*

This recipe continues the South American theme of the Caipirinha. As with the Caipirinha, be wary of the seemingly innocuous citric flavour. The proportions in this drink dictate that it is *strong*.

Pisco, for the uninitiated, is a clear brandy from Chile or Peru. It is clear because, unlike most brandies, Pisco is not aged in wood, and it is from the wood (plus the odd dash of caramel) that brandy derives its colour. In some parts, though it is becoming increasingly rare, Pisco is still stored in earthenware pots buried in the ground.

If you don't have special Sour glasses, Highball glasses will more than suffice. In your chosen glass, dissolve the sugar syrup or icing sugar in lemon juice. Pour in your Pisco and stir. Add three or four ice cubes and stir again. Decorate with a slice of lemon.

Y E L L O W   F I N G E R S

- *30 ml (1 fl oz) Southern Comfort*
- *15 ml ('/₂ fl oz) Galliano*
- *30 ml (1 fl oz) vodka*
- *30 ml (1 fl oz) orange juice*
- *Top up with chilled lemonade*
- *Slice of orange*

Here's a chance to mix the peach flavour of Southern Comfort with the liquorice of Galliano with a strong supporting cast.

Give the ingredients a thorough shake with some ice and pour into a Highball glass. Top up with lemonade and decorate with orange.

NON-ALCOHOLIC
COCKTAILS

BOO BOO'S SPECIAL

- *85 ml (3 fl oz) pineapple juice*
- *85 ml (3 fl oz) orange juice*
- *15 ml ('/₂ fl oz) lemon juice*
- *Dash of grenadine*
- *Dash of Angostura bitters*
- *Top up with chilled water (sparkling if preferred)*
- *Slice of pineapple*
- *Maraschino cherry*

Shake the fruit juices, grenadine and bitters thoroughly and pour over ice cubes in a Highball or Collins glass. Top up with water and decorate with a pineapple slice and maraschino cherry. It tastes as good as it sounds.

CARDINAL PUNCH

- *125 ml (4 fl oz) cranberry juice*
- *50 ml (2 fl oz) orange juice*
- *30 ml (1 fl oz) lemon juice*
- *Top up with chilled ginger ale*
- *Slices of orange and lemon*

Pour the fruit juices into a cocktail glass and stir before topping up with ginger ale. Decorate the side of the glass with the orange and lemon slices.

NURSERY FIZZ

- *125 ml (4 fl oz) orange juice*
- *125 ml (4 fl oz) ginger ale*
- *Slice of orange*
- *Maraschino cherry*

To demonstrate that simplicity can be sensational. Pour the orange juice and ginger ale into a large goblet. Decorate with orange slice and a cherry.

MULLED GRAPE AND APPLE PUNCH

- *1 apple tea bag*
- *2 cloves*
- *2 cinnamon sticks*
- *150 ml (5 fl oz) boiling water*
- *Pinch of grated nutmeg*
- *85 ml (3 fl oz) apple juice*
- *85 ml (3 fl oz) grape juice*
- *Slices of apple*

A winter warmer without the alcohol. Place the tea bag in a heatproof jug, then add the cloves and one cinnamon stick. Pour over the water and leave to infuse for 5 minutes, then discard the tea bag and spices.

Sprinkle the nutmeg over and mix in the fruit juices. Pour into a heatproof goblet. Serve decorated with a cinnamon stick stirrer and apple slices.

PRINCESS MARGARET

- *6 large strawberries*
- *Slice of pineapple*
- *Juice of ¹/₂ orange*
- *Juice of ¹/₂ lemon*
- *2 dashes of fraise (strawberry syrup)*
- *Sugar*

Blend ingredients with some cracked ice cubes in a blender until frothy. You can crown this royal extravaganza with fraise-soaked sugar frosting around the rim of a Highball glass, decorated with a strawberry.

ROSY PIPPIN

- *125 ml (4 fl oz) apple juice*
- *5 ml (1 tsp) lemon juice*
- *Dash of grenadine*
- *Top up with chilled ginger ale*
- *Slice of apple*

Pour ingredients into a Highball glass with some ice and stir. Top up with ginger ale and decorate with an apple slice.

TEMPERANCE MOCKTAIL

- *Juice of 1 lemon*
- *1 egg yolk*
- *2 dashes of grenadine*
- *Maraschino cherry*

What better way to conclude a cocktail book than with a chilled reminder of the days of American Prohibition? Give ingredients a thorough shake with ice and strain into a chilled cocktail glass. Decorate with a maraschino cherry. Cheers!

CREDITS

The Publishers would like to thank the
following for their help in producing this book:

THE OCEAN ROOMS, BRIGHTON
For providing a ready supply of the various
alcoholic drinks required to make the
cocktails, as well as some of the essential
tools and equipment needed to make the
drinks, featured in the photographs.
Also for lending us their excellent bartender,
Phil Harradence, who mixed and shook
all the drinks.

DIVERTIMENTI, LONDON
For providing the equipment used for
photography in The Essential Cocktail Kit
section on pages 8 to 11.

index